SEARCH FOR THE SPHINX

HIST SP ES

Jo Foster has
discovered tha
in 1980s Esse
she has made
programmes ii
Team and *Who*

If I was a kid wi
my guide. She
both the past a
has a mischievous sense of humour that would keep me
smiling throughout my journey.

Tony Robinson

Also by Jo Foster

SEARCH FOR THE SPHINX

HISTORY SPIES

JO FOSTER

ILLUSTRATED BY SCOULAR ANDERSON

MACMILLAN CHILDREN'S BOOKS

First published 2009 by Macmillan Children's Books
a division of Macmillan Publishers Limited
20 New Wharf Road, London N1 9RR
Basingstoke and Oxford
Associated companies throughout the world
www.panmacmillan.com

ISBN 978-0-330-44903-8

1 3 5 7 9 8 6 4 2

A CIP catalogue record for this book is available from the British Library.

Typeset by Perfect Bound Ltd
Printed and bound in the UK by CPI Mackays, Chatham ME5 8TD

The Publisher would like to thank the following for permission to reproduce material.
Every care has been taken to trace copyright holders. However, if there have been
unintentional omissions or failure to trace copyright holders, we apologize and will,
if informed, endeavour to make corrections in any future edition.
Page 89 The Art Archive/Luxor Museum/Gianni Dagli Orti

So you're the new kid.

Have you ever been on a top-secret, life-and-death, time-bending government mission before?

Well, I have. I've been on loads. I'm Charlie Cartwright, History Spy, Super-Snooper, Clock-Defier and Master of Disguise! And all since last year. Let me tell you a true story . . .

1

Once upon a time, my life was almost as boring as yours.

Then on my birthday last year, I got a phone call: it was a bloke from the Department for Historical Accuracy. See, the government had invented a way to go back in time. They wanted someone to travel around and check up on what really happened in history. And they picked me. Probably because of my astounding talents and unusually large brain, I expect.

Since then I've been travelling through time, spying on the craziest stuff. Battles and magicians and feasts and duels. All sorts!

And now you're coming along too, and you're with the best guide around. I'll make sure you get to see everything that's worth seeing!

I'll show you what to wear, what to eat, where to go, how people have fun, where they live – everything. Stick with me and almost nothing can go wrong.

Department for Historical Accuracy

HISTORY SPY 00001
NAME CHARLIE CARTWRIGHT
CLEARANCE ULTRA

Pass must be carried at all times when on official missions. Not valid without stamp.

HISTORY SPIES · ACCURACY · DEPARTMENT · FOR · HISTORICAL ·

Our next top-secret History Spy mission is to...

EGYPT
1333 BC

If you want to be a History Spy you have to learn to be invisible. It's not magic – the best way to be invisible is to look just like everyone else.

In some places it's better to look ordinary:

But in other places, ordinary is downright weird.

Here, you can share my extremely confidential History Spies' Fact File. It's all important stuff cos it'll help you go unnoticed. And that could save your life.

5

Clothes are very important. If you turned up in Ancient Egypt wearing what you've got on now, they'd think you were some kind of alien.

DRESS LIKE YOUR MUMMY

If you want to dress as an Egyptian for a fancy-dress party, it's easy: all you need is one loo roll.

But that's not going to cut it for undercover work. Egyptians might make a lot of mummies, but they don't want to see them wandering around.

It can be quite easy to dress as an Egyptian kid – as long as you're not shy. In hot weather, girls and boys sometimes go around with no clothes on at all!

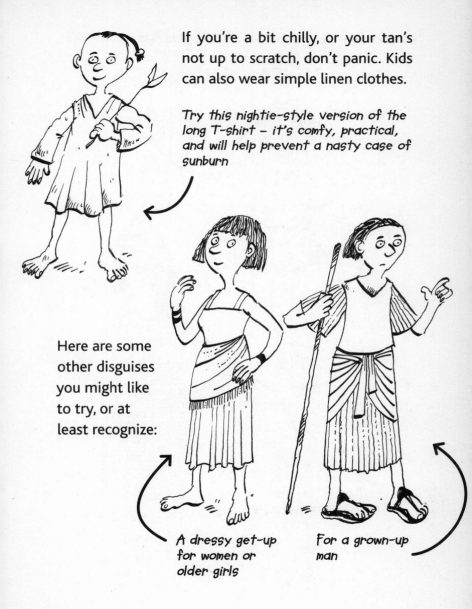

If you're a bit chilly, or your tan's not up to scratch, don't panic. Kids can also wear simple linen clothes.

Try this nightie-style version of the long T-shirt – it's comfy, practical, and will help prevent a nasty case of sunburn

Here are some other disguises you might like to try, or at least recognize:

A dressy get-up for women or older girls

For a grown-up man

This is for a man who's got work to do – or maybe he just can't afford many clothes!

It does occasionally get a bit nippy in Egypt. You can always throw on a little cape

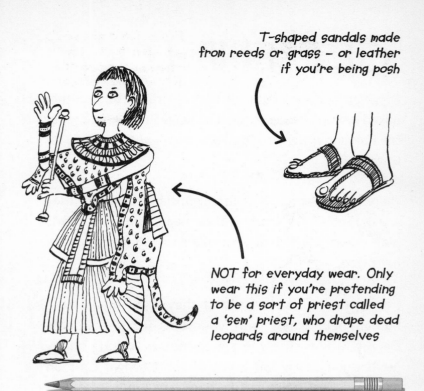

T-shaped sandals made from reeds or grass – or leather if you're being posh

NOT for everyday wear. Only wear this if you're pretending to be a sort of priest called a 'sem' priest, who drape dead leopards around themselves

Attention: History Spies

Archaeologists don't yet know everything about what Egyptians wore. They're a bit confused about whether people actually wore the same kinds of clothes you see in paintings and statues or not. On your mission in Egypt, please draw what people are wearing and make plenty of notes to bring back to the Department.

GET THE LOOK

Egyptian clothes aren't all that exciting. You're either naked or you're wearing a bit of beige linen. It's time for the hair and make-up – that's where Egyptians really go to town.

There's a special hairstyle that Egyptian kids wear – they shave the hair off most of their head, but leave a long plait down one side. If your hair's too short, try a fake hairpiece.

The Egyptians love wigs, and they're all made from human hair. Bored with your do? Try the 'Double Decker', a two-storey wig with masses of long skinny plaits underneath and a riot of short brown curls on top. Wild! Feel free just to whack a wig on top of your real hair. But, like a lot of Egyptians, you might find it easier and more comfortable to shave off all your hair and then slip on a wig.

This is where it all gets a bit girly. We need to do our make-up before we go to Egypt, or we'll look like stinky scruffs.

Egyptians won't leave the house without their moisturizer. Try a bit of oil rubbed into your skin. It's not just a beauty cream: the weather in Egypt is so hot and dry that if you don't keep your skin oiled it will shrivel up and crack, and you could get a serious infection. Tough manly builders get moisturizer as part of their pay, and they have been known to go on strike if their potions don't get handed out on time. Look for scented oil if you can – the Egyptians can't get enough of strong perfume.

AUTOMATIC HAIR GEL

Archaeologists have found pictures like this of women wearing big cones of perfumed fat on top of their heads at parties, so that as the evening went on the fat would melt and they'd stay perfumed all night long. But would a young lady really want a lump of animal grease melting all over her hair, even if it did smell nice? Could this picture just be a sign that these girls are gorgeous, and they smell great too?

We're not sure.
History Spies should keep their eyes peeled for real-life examples of women melting lard on their heads.

And now for the really fun bit. I get to draw on you!
Close your eyes and hold very, very still ...

EYE CONTACT

It's time to borrow your big sister's eyeliner and get
practising – girls *and* boys. In Ancient Egypt, everyone
wears lots of black eyeliner. Carefully (don't poke your
eye out!) draw a thick black line on your top and bottom
eyelid, going out to the side like this:

In Egypt, you can't just buy an eye pencil from Boots.
They use a kind of paint called kohl, which you mix with
water and then paint on with a blunt stick.

It's not just because they like the goth look – wearing a big dark line of kohl protects your eyes from the glare of the sun, a bit like shades, and the Egyptians believe it prevents eye infections too.

Right – sandals, nightie, crazy hairdo up – you look almost r... Let's just have a quick check to make sure our costumes are right:

NO denim, Gore-tex or Lycra. Stick to linen cloth.

NO brightly coloured clothes. The Egyptians haven't got dyeing right yet.

NO attention-grabbing hair. If yours is blond, ginger, or bright green, shave it all off!

Before we go, there's more to learn so that you don't do something stupid and give us away. Pay attention to . . .

THE VITAL BACKGROUND BRIEFING

The essential quick-reference guide for any History Spy travelling to Ancient Egypt. Keep this with you at all times!

MAP

POPULATION : roughly 3–4 million

MAIN CITIES:

THEBES The religious capital of Egypt, where royal mummies are buried in the Valley of the Kings.

MEMPHIS The main capital, where the Pharaoh rules from.

AMARNA The town where Tutankhamen grew up. Built not long ago by oddball Pharaoh Akhenaten. After he died, everyone left town.

GIZA Where the ancient Pyramids and the Sphinx are. Good for a spot of sightseeing.

Watch out – don't ask the way to Cairo. It doesn't exist yet.

I really want to go to Thebes — but we could have a peek at the Pyramids on the way, I reckon.

Egypt is a long, thin country, because people can only live near the River Nile. That's where all the water is, and the only place food can grow. The Egyptians don't call it the Nile though — to them, it's just 'the river', because it's the only one they care about!

BE *SUN-SAFE* !

Egypt gets really hot, especially around midday. If you've got pale skin or you're not used to the sun, cover up outdoors or sneak in some sunscreen.

The sun is so strong in Egypt that they worship it as a god – see pages 89–90. In fact, the weather rules everything. Farmers can only grow anything after the Nile has flooded, which happens once a year. The water rises and then falls again, leaving a thick layer of black sticky mud that's perfect for planting seeds in. Everyone watches the height of the Nile very carefully. If it stays too low, nothing will grow and there won't be enough to eat all year. But if it goes too high, you could be waving goodbye to your house.

GETTING AROUND

BY RIVER : The Nile isn't just important for growing food, it's also Egypt's version of the motorway. There aren't really any roads, and because most of the places you'll want to get to are close to the river, it makes sense to go by boat.

The Egyptians have two different words for 'travelling', depending on whether you're going north or south. It shows how important the riverboats are to them. If you're going south, you can put your sail up and use the wind which always blows from north to south. So the word for going south uses this picture:

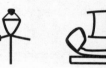

travel upstream
(southward)

When you come back, the wind's going against you – but the Nile current flows from south to north so you can use your oars to row along easily. So the word for going north uses this picture:

travel downstream
(northward)

DONKEY WORK: If you need to carry lots of heavy grain around, away from the river, your best bet is to get hold of a donkey and load it up with bags. There aren't any camels in Egypt yet!

CUTTING-EDGE CHARIOTS: The first horses only turned up in Egypt fairly recently. You almost certainly won't get to ride one, unless you're a close friend of the Pharaoh and other royal types who keep a few exotic horses to pull their chariots.

FOOT POWER: For most people, the only way to get around over land is to walk. If you're rich and lazy, you can get some servants to carry you around in a box called a litter.

STAYING HEALTHY

History Spies should always make sure they get the right vaccinations before they travel back in time, and look after their health during missions. Remember: you're no use to the Department if you're ill.

There are several dangerous animals in Egypt. The River Nile is an especially risky place. Remember that crocodiles and hippos like to hang out in the same places where humans like to go swimming, and they both have powerful jaws. There are also parasitic worms in the river which can lay eggs inside you, and cause a nasty disease called bilharzia.

If you develop a cough, get it checked out as soon as possible. Tuberculosis and bronchitis are widespread in Egypt, because living in damp mud huts gives people weak chests. Eating dirty or undercooked food often gives History Spies in Egypt nasty stomach bugs, as well as parasites like tapeworms and liver flukes.

Both snakes and scorpions are common and can be poisonous – watch where you step!

Luckily, Egyptian medicine is very advanced for its time. If you break a bone or have a similar simple injury in Egypt, you should be fine with a surgeon. However, some Egyptian remedies are pretty useless, and are only good for helping you to fit in with the ordinary Egyptians who use them.

For instance, you could wear the symbol of the eye of Horus. The story goes that the god Horus had his eye knocked out by his uncle Seth, and then it was healed by another god – so it's a good symbol to wear if you want to be healed. And to protect yourself from being bitten by snakes and scorpions at night, you could keep a magic wand made from hippopotamus ivory under your bed. At least that's less unpleasant than this Egyptian cure for baldness: you take a bone from the spine of a rook, a burnt hoof from a donkey, and the fat from a black snake. Mix it all up and rub it on your head.

I suppose if you went out in public stinking of that, at least people wouldn't be thinking, 'Hey, look at the bald guy!' They'd be holding their noses and running away!

MONEY

Buying things in Ancient Egypt can be extremely confusing. The Egyptians don't use money! If you want a duck to eat for your dinner, you have to have something you can swap for it. And if you have a job, you won't be paid in cash at the end of the week – you'll get a pile of bread and beer!

There are some things it's easier to swap. History Spies should make sure they always have plenty of the following:

- **SILVER**

- **COPPER**

- **GRAIN**

- **OIL**

There are standard weights of each of these items which you can use as a price – so you might be able to buy something with five grams of silver, for instance. Merchants should have little stones of a certain size to weigh things out with. In general, you should be prepared to bargain hard whenever you buy anything – this can be very tiring if you're not used to it!

I don't mind this. I think it's quite cool that no one has any money. It makes buying dinner a bit of a game. Shame they don't like swapping stickers. I'd be rolling in it if they did!

WHAT TIME IS IT?

The Egyptians have hours, days, months and years like we do, but no minutes or seconds – just 'moments'. So if you're a few minutes late for an appointment, the chances are no one will notice.

Each day is 24 hours, like in our time – 12 hours of day and 12 hours of night. But a week is 10 days long, not 7, which would make you look forward to the one-day weekend even more. There are 30 days in every month, and 12 months in every year, plus an extra 5 days at the end of every year to make it up to 365 days.

There are 3 seasons in the Egyptian year:

AKHET – when the Nile floods

PERET – when you plant seeds in the sticky mud so they've got enough water to grow

SHEMU – drought – when it's hot and dry

The problem is that there aren't actually 365 days in a year, there are 365¼. That's why we have leap years – because otherwise, the days get all behind themselves like a clock running slow, and before you know it it's winter in July and you're having barbecues for New Year's Eve. The Egyptians know something's up, because as well as their normal calendars they have religious calendars which go by the moon, and farming festivals which go by the sun, so they can tell how long a year is really supposed to be. But instead of changing it, they just let their seasons get in a right mess. If you want to know for sure what season it's going to be when you get to Egypt, you're going to have to do some tricky maths.

And remember, if you say it's 1333 BC, no one will have a clue what you mean. Our 'BC' years count forward to the birth of Jesus Christ, and of course the Egyptians aren't sitting around waiting for him to turn up. Instead, they count their years as the first, fourth, or whatever of the Pharaoh's reign.

I think we're heading for the third year of Tutankhamen. It's pretty hard to tell though because no one can really agree on the date!

PHRASEBOOK

Historians and archaeologists have had trouble working out how some Egyptian words should sound, because when Egyptians wrote things down they didn't use any vowels, only consonants.

Try filling in the vowels in this:

CN Y NDRSTND THS SNTNC?
MYB – BT F Y DDN'T SPK NGLSH,
T WLD B RLLY CNFSNG!

Imagine how much harder it would be if you had no idea what the words were supposed to sound like in the first place.

Because of this, the Department for Historical Accuracy has specially trained agents researching the language of Ancient Egypt. We give all our History Spies excellent language training, but occasionally there are still things we don't know.

Here are a few Egyptian words you might come across:

ANKH – life. This is the hieroglyph for 'ankh', which you'll often see used as a good luck symbol.

DESHRET – the desert outside Egypt. Deshret means 'Red Land'.

ITERU – the river (the Nile)

KEMET – Egypt. It means 'Black Land', or the country close to the Nile where the ground is made of black mud.

MA'AT – truth, order and harmony. A very important thing for the tidy-minded Egyptians!

MEDJAT – roll of papyrus, like a book

MER – pyramid

MERI – to love

NEFER – good

NEMES – the headdress a king wears. Much lighter and more practical than a crown.

NETJER – god

NIWT – city. You might hear Thebes called 'niwt' – it's so famous, people just call it 'the city'!

PER – house

SESH – scribe. Special people with the magical powers of reading and writing (see p. 77).

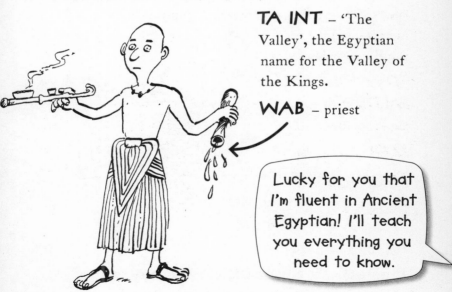

TA INT – 'The Valley', the Egyptian name for the Valley of the Kings.

WAB – priest

Lucky for you that I'm fluent in Ancient Egyptian! I'll teach you everything you need to know.

CODENAME : MR BIG

Of course, you'll need to pick an Egyptian name — strange foreign names will only draw attention to you. Egyptians are given names by their mums as soon as they're born, so they often have soppy meanings like 'She belongs to me' (Aneksi). Sometimes, though, kids are named for what they look like. So if you were a huge bouncing baby boy, you might have the name Wersu, which means 'He's big'. Here are a few more you could go for:

Nakht = Strong

Nofret = Beautiful

Meru = Beloved

Pakapu = The bird catcher

Mersure = May Re love him

Senetenpu = It is our sister

Pakamen = The blind one

Pakharu = The Syrian

Panehsy = The Nubian (Nubia's a country south of Egypt, about where Sudan is today)

Egyptians believe that without your name, you don't really exist – which is why mums give names to their kids as soon as they can. And if there's someone you don't like, you can hurt them with a very simple spell: just write their name down on an old pot, then smash the pot. Even if the magic doesn't work, it might make you feel better!

People often have two names, a long name and a nickname.

But if you're king, you get a tongue-twisting *five*. Tutankhamen's full name, and its meaning, is:

Ka-nakht tut-mesut   *'Strong bull, fitting of created forms'*

Nefer-hepu segereh-tawy sehetep-netjeru nebu
        'Dynamic of laws, who calms the Two Lands, who pleases all the gods'

Wetjes-khau sehetep-netjeru
        'He displays the regalia, he pleases the gods'

Nebkheprure   *'The royal manifestation of Re'*

Tutankhamen heqa-Iunu-shema
        'Living image of Amun, ruler of Upper Egyptian Heliopolis'

Bit of a mouthful. I wonder if he ever forgets any of them?

TAKE ME TO YOUR LEADER

Everyone knows the rulers of Egypt are called the Pharaohs. Pharaohs have been in charge in Egypt for more than 1,500 years, and they're not going anywhere any time soon.

Pharaoh owns the whole country and everyone in it! The Egyptians believe that Pharaoh is the son of Amun, the all-powerful sun god. Pharaoh has a hotline to the gods, so if the Egyptians want to stay safe, they have to keep being nice to him.

Everyone has to do whatever the Pharaoh tells them, and for a certain time every year you have to stop doing your normal job and do work for the Pharaoh instead. He might have a pyramid he wants building, or a canal that needs digging – and no one gets out of it with a note from their mum. If you want to avoid it, you'll have to be rich enough to pay for someone else to do your work instead of you.

Don't worry, no one's going to make US build any pyramids! I think we're a bit weedy for that anyway . . . no offence.

Tutankhamen is the latest Pharaoh. He's just got on to the throne and though you probably think of him as a dusty old mummy, he's still a kid in the year you're travelling to. He was only 8 or 9 when the last Pharaoh died and Tut got power. But poor old Tut hasn't got very long to go as ruler of Egypt – he'll die when he's about 17 or 18.

Because Tut's only little, he's not quite the real boss yet. There's a man called Ay who tells him what to do. After Tutankhamen dies, Ay will be Pharaoh for a short while. The real cause of Tutankhamen's death is still a mystery, but some people think that Ay got jealous and murdered Tutankhamen so *he* could be in charge instead.

There's another important guy around called Horemheb. He's head of the army at the moment, which is a pretty good job, but that's not all. After Ay's had a go, Horemheb will have his turn at being Pharaoh.

After all this, Tutankhamen gets pretty much forgotten for a few thousand years – he's only a kid, and he doesn't get to do very much. But in your time, he's one of the most famous Pharaohs around. That's because he was buried in a hidden tomb that managed to escape being cleared out by robbers. That meant that when it was discovered in the 1920s it was the most impressive thing anyone had seen in ages.

And we might get to see him before he's a mummy!

HOW TO SPOT A PHARAOH

If you're lucky enough to meet Pharaoh, you'll need to recognize who he is so that you can do enough grovelling – it's best to throw yourself face-down on the ground if you bump into him. Look out for the following signs:

HEADGEAR : The Pharaoh has several different crowns, but they're a bit of a hassle to wear every day. He'll usually be wearing a stripy cloth on his head, tied with a headband, with a snake on the front facing out. The snake is the Number 1 way to spot a pharaoh – it's a cobra, which is supposed to spit poison to keep the Pharaoh's enemies away.

That's pretty cool. I want a hat that can poison people! No one would mess with me!

STICKS: The Pharaoh carries two special sticks, a shepherd's crook and a sort of flyswat.

HAIRY: Almost everyone else in Egypt shaves, but the Pharaoh wears a beard, just like the gods. It doesn't have to be a real beard. A few years ago, there was a woman pharaoh named Hatshepsut. She was obviously more bothered about looking god-like than looking pretty, because in all the pictures of her she's wearing a false beard!

THE LAW

Pharaoh's not powerful just because he's a god. He's got some really horrible punishments up his sleeve if anyone steps out of line. Be careful not to get caught committing any crimes, or you could find yourself made a slave in a work gang, beaten, having your face permanently scarred, or – the most horrible punishment of all – being held over a sharp wooden post and dropped. The post goes all the way through you, but you don't die straightaway.

As far as the Egyptians are concerned, being made into a live kebab isn't even the worst punishment they can imagine. The stuff they're really afraid of is being drowned or burned alive – both of those stop your family from keeping your dead body, and that means you can't live on in the afterlife like everyone else will.

I don't fancy any of those at all. Please please PLEASE don't get us caught if we accidentally do anything illegal!

Finally, let's run through a few things you must never, ever do in Ancient Egypt, if you don't want to be caught out.

DO watch out for crocodiles and hippos if you go for a swim in the Nile.

DON'T touch the Pharaoh if you happen to spot him – it's not allowed, and you DON'T want to make Pharaoh angry!

DON'T let people see you making notes in English – the Egyptians have a couple of types of writing, but none of it uses our letters.

Got it? Good. We've done enough homework – let's get going and find out what it was really like!

So here we are – Ancient Egypt. Are you OK? We just travelled back more than three thousand years, so you might feel a bit jetlagged for a while!

It's a totally different world here. Can you believe we're going to be hanging out with the people who built the pyramids?

In fact, that reminds me. I want to do some sightseeing first so I brought us out to Giza. If we just walk over this sand dune we should see ... WOW!

WWWWWWWWWWWWWWWWWWWWWWMMMMMMMMMMMMMMMMMMM

THE PYRAMIDS

Even though you've travelled back through history more than three thousand years, the Pyramids are *still* ancient. Even in 1333, the Pyramids at Giza were built more than a thousand years ago.

The first pyramids in Egypt were the first big stone buildings anywhere, ever. They were built to last, because they were where the Pharaohs were buried, and people believed that if they led a good life and were buried in the right way they'd live forever in the afterlife.

The smooth outer layer of stone on the Pyramids will wear away over the thousands of years after they

The pyramids in our time

were built – but even then, their size alone makes them some of the most impressive buildings on the planet. The Great Pyramid, built by the Pharaoh Khufu, is the biggest of the lot. It's nearly 150 metres high and it's mostly solid lumps of stone, with a few rooms and passageways inside it. It's as tall as twenty-eight giraffes standing on each other's heads, or one-and-a-half Statues of Liberty!

I can't believe how huge they are. It's amazing that the Egyptians built them before they'd invented trucks, cranes, diggers . . .

It's the size of the Pyramids that first hits you, but it's just as impressive that the Egyptians managed to build them so *neatly*. The Great Pyramid at Giza is laid out almost exactly along a north–south line, and its massive base is gobsmackingly level, with only a 2cm difference between the highest and lowest bits. The outer stones on the Pyramids are fitted together so perfectly that you can't even fit a knife blade between them.

And what gadgets did the Egyptians use to check their straight lines and level ground? Mostly some very simple wooden tools and some really long bits of string. But they did it so well, you can almost see why some people think they must have had help from super-intelligent aliens.

The amount of stone that had to be heaved into place is also pretty unbelievable. The Great Pyramid has more than two million blocks, each of which weighed two and a half tonnes – which is half a smallish African elephant, or about seventy eleven-year-old kids! How could they possibly shift stones that huge to the top of a pyramid without using mechanical cranes? The answer is, they only raised each block a bit at a time. When they'd built as high as they could, they made a slope up to the next level so that they could roll the stones to the top and keep working upward. Then, when they'd got to the top, they smoothed over the outsides and took down the ramps as they worked their way down the Pyramid.

ROLL OVER

How did the Pyramid builders manage to move enormous blocks of stone to where they were needed?

Historians are still not sure exactly how the Egyptians built the Pyramids, though History Spies are of course investigating. We do know that they use sledges to drag big lumps of stone across smoothed-out tracks. Egyptian builders have also been spotted using rollers to move heavy weights. You can see how by trying your own pyramid-building experiment.

Start with something heavy and squarish to use as a sledge. Try a hardback book, with the things you want to move stacked on top of it. You'll also need a handful of pencils or crayons, all the same thickness. Lay the pencils alongside each other on a hard floor and sit the book on top of them. Now, if you push the book along, you'll find it moves easily over the rolling pencils. If you don't have hundreds of pencils, you can make the line longer by picking up the pencils from the back end of the book, putting them down in front again, and carrying on

I guess if we wanted to try that, we'd probably need to find ourselves a few hundred workers as well . . .

from there. This technique works for moving all kinds of things – even huge heavy bits of stone, if you use tree trunks instead of pencils, and pour mud over them to keep things running smoothly.

TRUE OR FALSE?

The
Pyramids were
built by thousands of slaves,
who were whipped by their cruel
overseers to keep them working
till they dropped.

A big fat FALSE. It's true that the workers were told they had to work for Pharaoh, but they were still free after they'd done their work and they got paid for it. In fact they were pretty well looked after.

PYRAMIDS – WHAT'S THE POINT?

The Pyramids are so impressive that people have come up with all kinds of strange theories about why they were built. Do any of these sound likely to you?

The pyramid shape itself has special powers. Just putting a dead king inside a pyramid would preserve his body. You can also make food last longer by putting it under a cardboard pyramid, or keep razor blades sharp by keeping them under a pyramid shape.

> Hmm. Wouldn't that mean that Toblerones would last forever?

The three Pyramids at Giza were deliberately built to match up with the positions of the stars in Orion's belt, because a bunch of very ancient clever-clogses really liked astronomy.

The Great Pyramid was actually built as a power station, using futuristic nuclear fission technology to send energy to Mars. Aliens taught the Egyptians to build the Pyramids, so they could get the power.

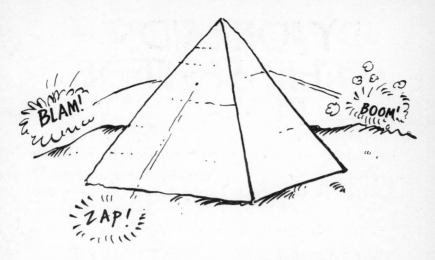

Whether it was humans or aliens who designed it, **the Great Pyramid was really a gigantic weapon of mass destruction.** It could fire rays that would cause a nuclear explosion, or cook an enemy instantly with raging heat.

The Egyptians didn't come up with the idea for the Pyramid on their own – **God told them to do it.**

The Pyramids were built as homes for dead Pharaohs, where they could live forever. A pyramid's sides slope up to the sky so that the king's spirit can walk up it to heaven.

Hang on – I think that last one's supposed to be true. It still sounds pretty silly to me!

RIDDLE OF THE SPHINX

Now this is something really special. If you've ever seen pictures of the Sphinx before, it's time for a game of Spot the Difference . . .

The Sphinx is a mythical Egyptian monster, a lion with the head of a man. It represents the king's power, and it's probably supposed to be guarding all the dead kings inside their pyramids. All the modern pictures of the Sphinx show it with its nose missing.

Historians have no idea when the Sphinx's nose fell off. It had gone by the time Europeans saw it in the 1700s – but before then, we have no idea. There's a rumour that a religious guy in the fourteenth century might have lopped it off, but whatever the truth, the nose has never been found. Any History Spies travelling back far enough in time to see the whole of the Sphinx's face should bring as many pictures as possible back to the Department.

The Sphinx's nose . . . that would make an amazing souvenir. I guess we'd have trouble lugging it around though – it's probably about as tall as I am!

> We're not just here for ancient sightseeing though. The Pyramids are old news. These days, the happening place to be is further down the river, around Thebes. Come on – we'll hop on a boat!

PLAIN SAILING

The Egyptians are so obsessed with travelling by boat that they have more than 100 different words for all the types they have. And because the sun manages to travel all the way across the sky every day, they think it *must* be a god going by boat. How else would he be able to do it?

> This is so much better than sitting in a car on a motorway to get from A to B! It's not so hot when you're on the river with a gentle breeze . . . so relaxing . . . ZZZZZZZZZZZZZZ

Speech bubble: What? Did I miss something? Oh, we're here already! Sorry – sightseeing always makes me sleepy.

THEBES – CITY OF THE GODS

Thebes isn't the capital of Egypt – the government is in Memphis in northern Egypt – but it's the most holy city in Egypt, and it's very important for the Pharaohs of the Eighteenth Dynasty, the set Tutankhamen belongs to.

On the east side of the Nile, there are two main parts to Thebes. There's an enormous temple, and next door is the city where people actually live and work.

Across the river on the west side is something that sounds much more romantic – the Valley of the Kings!

GRAVES FIT FOR PHARAOHS

The Egyptians haven't built pyramids to bury their kings in for nearly 200 years now. The problem with pyramids was they were too easy to break into, so they kept on getting burgled. After all, if you're going to leave pots of gold and valuables with only a dead man to look after them, it's probably best not to make it even more obvious by building a whopping great shiny pyramid on top. So these days, the kings are buried in underground tombs cut straight into the rocks near Thebes. They still have plenty of precious goodies buried with them, and even though they're supposed to be hidden, they still get cleared out by determined burglars.

And I've got a friend who lives just down the road from the Valley of the Kings. Come on, let's go and see him.

VISITING MERYRE

Hey, Charlie — thanks for coming! Come on in. Everyone's out so you can have a look round the house.

We've painted the walls white. Otherwise it gets very hot in the middle of the day.

In the hall we have lots of statues of our favourite gods, so we can have a word with them whenever we like. My job is to leave food for them.

HOW TO BUILD
AN EGYPTIAN HOUSE

If you're staying in Ancient Egypt for a while on a mission, you may want to build yourself a house. You'll need to start by making some mud bricks.

- First, take some nice gloopy Nile mud and a few good handfuls of straw.

- Chop up the straw and stir it into the mud.

- Put the gloop into a wooden mould and leave it to dry in the sun. Now you're ready to go!

Mud-brick houses are cheap and easy to build, but the problem is they're breakable and they fall down quite often. When they do, people just pull them down and build new ones on top of the piles of rubble – so Egyptian towns keep on rising higher and higher.

This means that archaeologists back in our time don't know as much as they'd like about Ancient Egyptian towns and villages. There aren't many left. However, modern historians know a lot about Egyptian tombs, because they were built of stone and meant to last forever. Because of this, History Spies should take every chance to go into ordinary houses and send plenty of notes back to the Department for Historical Accuracy.

A GOOD NIGHT'S SLEEP

Most Egyptians just sleep on mats, on the floor or on raised brick platforms. Some have pretty good beds though, with linen strips fastened at each end to a wooden frame to form a sling shape. History Spies may have trouble getting used to Egyptian pillows, which are made of wood. You can wrap them in a sheet to make them a bit more comfy.

Remember: NEVER start a pillow fight with an Egyptian. I learned that one the hard way!

THE GREAT GOD MOG

People don't usually give their pet cats names, but they do think they're divine.

The goddess Bastet is a cat with the power to protect people. At the moment she's mainly worshipped just in the city of Bubastis, but later on there will be a family of kings from Bubastis who make her popular all over Egypt. There will even be whole cemeteries of cats. People pay to have their cats mummified as a prayer to Bastet.

I've got a cat at home and she already thinks she's a goddess. I'm not telling her about all this – her head would get so big it wouldn't fit through the cat flap!

FOUR~LEGGED FRIENDS

History Spies can sometimes get lonely on missions far from home. If you're staying in Ancient Egypt for a while, why not get a pet? Pets are popular with all sorts of Egyptians. But do your homework: if you're in disguise as a poor farmer you'll arouse suspicion if you take a leopard for a walk.

MONKEY : A cheeky, friendly pet that's fun for all the family. Too pricey for poor people to keep.

DOG : Egypt's favourite pet, in spite of everything you've heard about cats. Just like in your time, dogs are great company for people. And what with all the bread and beer the Egyptians make at home, they need dogs around to help keep rats out of their grain stores.

BIRD : You could pick several different kinds of bird for a pet, but if you want one that looks gorgeous, is brightly coloured and is easy to tame, go for a hoopoe.

> Makes a nice change from a budgie, I suppose, but surely there's something more exciting?

EXOTIC WILDLIFE :

Pharaohs and other very rich people can buy all sorts of animals from around Africa to keep as pets. Ever fancied riding an ostrich? Grooming a giraffe? Tickling a leopard's tummy? Now's your chance.

> Now, that's MUCH more like it!

And if your fluffy friend should get ill and die, don't just bury him at the bottom of the garden. If you can afford it, get Fido mummified! That way he'll live forever and you can go for walkies together in the afterlife.

PLAY TIME

Some Egyptian toys will look familiar to modern kids, such as rattles, toy animals and dolls. They're made out of wood rather than plastic, but are sometimes quite sophisticated. You can get animals with moving parts, like a crocodile that snaps its jaws. With luck, that toy would teach its owner to stay away from the river so as not to get snapped up.

There are also games which adults play and which History Spies should get to know.

Just like your auntie at Christmas, the Egyptians love playing board games. And luckily some of them are pretty easy to learn. Their favourite game for two people is called **SENET.**

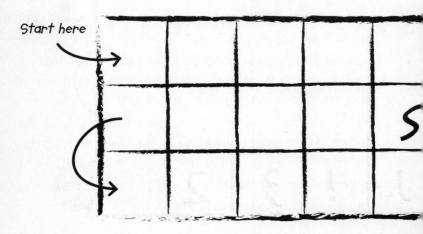

Start here

HOW TO PLAY SENET

YOU WILL NEED:

■ A board like this, with three rows of ten squares. You can buy fancy senet boards, or you can just draw one on a piece of papyrus or clay, or on the ground in chalk if you like.

■ Seven counters for each player. Make sure they're different colours or shapes so you can tell whose they are!

■ Something to use instead of dice, which the Egyptians don't have yet. They use five wooden sticks which are flattened on one side, so you throw them all and count how many land face-up. If you're practising the game at home before going to Egypt, use coins: throw five in the air and count how many land heads-up.

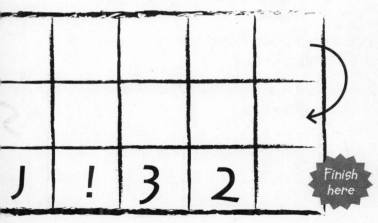

1. Line up the counters, alternating yours with your opponent's, in the first fourteen squares. The square S is now the point where the game begins.

2. Throw the sticks to get your score.

3. Choose which of your counters you want to move along the number of squares you've just scored. You CANNOT land on a square where your opponent already has a counter.

4. Keep taking turns like this, until one of the counters gets close to the squares with markings.

   J: The 'good' square – you're getting close to the finish line!

   $!$: DANGER SQUARE! If you land here, you have a choice: either stay here until you score an exact 4 to move your piece off, or go back to S and start again.

   3: You need to score exactly 3 to move your piece off the board.

   2: You need to score exactly 2 to move your piece off the board.

The winner is the first person to move all their pieces off the board.

If you can get some friends together and fancy trying an energetic Egyptian game, have a go at one of these:

TIP-CAT

Find two wooden sticks – one's the 'cat', the other's your bat. Throw the cat in the air and hit it as hard as you can with the bat – whoever can hit the cat furthest, wins. It's sort of like rounders, but without all that complicated running and catching business.

PRESSING THE GRAPES

Find either three or five friends and stand in a circle, holding hands. Don't start any namby-pamby ring-a-ring-o'-roses nonsense – and make sure you're holding on tight. Every alternate person should lean back as far as possible, lifting their toes off the ground and digging their heels in, while the others stay standing up. Then start spinning round in your star shape, as fast as you can without falling over. Dizziness guaranteed.

I have no idea how they manage to do that in this heat! I need a sit-down and a drink of water . . .

TUG OF WAR

You might have played this before, but for the Egyptian version you don't even need a rope. You'll need to line up two teams of people, with the team captains at the front of the lines, facing each other. The captains stand close together with their toes touching, grab on to each other's wrists, and lean back. Their teammates have to grab on to them by the waist in a long chain, and then PULL. You can see why you need a captain with a good grip!

Kids also enjoy swimming – you don't have to pay to go to a pool, you just jump in the nearest canal. There are plenty of them, to take water to the fields.

That sounds great! I bet chariot-racing is more exciting than go-karting back in our time. Royal kids get all the fun.

Some lucky kids grow up in the royal court, alongside the Pharaoh's sons. Lots of the games they play are all about learning to fight in wars, so they're even more violent than the tug of war. They spend their time practising archery, driving chariots, wrestling, and fighting with sticks.

Thanks for the game, guys! You must be hungry. Come in and have some lunch – we've got plenty.

Remember – there aren't any knives and forks, so it's fine to eat with your fingers. But wash your hands first. I don't want you getting ill on me!

Bread

Beans

Boiled fish

Leeks

To drink: beer for grown-ups, milk or water for kids

This is a decent meal, because Meryre's dad has a good job. Poor people in Ancient Egypt often just live off bread and a few lentils, with beer to drink. Any History Spies who are heavy-boned or a bit chubby should either lose weight before travelling to Egypt or make sure they're disguised as a rich person. High-class people are the only ones who can afford to eat enough meat, pastries and honey to get fat!

YOU ARE WHAT YOU EAT

... and if that's true, Ancient Egyptians are made of 99% bread! I don't mind it, but after a while I start craving a big bowl of pasta or a nice heap of cheesy mash.

It's true that there are over forty names for different kinds of bread, cakes and biscuits in Egypt. Most people eat bread every day. History Spies should mind their teeth if they're going to be staying in Egypt for a while: the bread almost always has tiny bits of stone and whole uncrushed grains mixed in with the flour, and that grinds your teeth away pretty quickly. If Egyptians live to an old age, they usually end up with very stubby teeth because of this!

But it's not all bread. For rich Egyptians, there are all sorts of foods available in Tutankhamen's time. If you know where to get it, you could feast on roast beef, fish, duck, rich goose, pigeon, pork, goat, and even gazelles and antelope! For your vitamins, make sure you get plenty of fruit and veg: try refreshing lettuce, garlic, onions, leeks, chickpeas, green peas, sticky dates, juicy pomegranates, grapes or raisins, cucumbers, olives and argun fruit – which tastes a bit like coconut.

Your food should also have plenty of flavour, because there are all sorts of spices around in Egypt, from mustard and thyme to cinnamon and aniseed. Don't look for the pepper grinder though – the Egyptians don't know about black pepper until the Greeks turn up in a few hundred years' time.

Be careful: there are plenty of things Egyptians don't eat for religious reasons. The problem is that these rules change depending on where and when you are in Egypt, and even who you are! People in one city might not eat a particular kind of fish, because their favourite local god likes to appear on earth as that fish and they wouldn't want to eat him by accident. But in another city, you could tuck right in. Some people won't eat pork because it's a special animal for the god Osiris. But that's mostly priests and some rich people. Poor people are usually less fussy: they'll eat pork if they can get hold of some!

The only safe thing is to follow what the people around you are eating, and to remember to check the rules extra carefully if you're disguised as a priest.

Sorry, but I have to go to work now. I'd ask you to come too, but I think my dad might get suspicious. Tell you what, come back next week – it's a holiday and we've all been looking forward to it for ages. See you then!

THE FAMILY BUSINESS

In Deir el-Medina, the village where Meryre lives, every day is Bring Your Kids To Work Day. Deir el-Medina isn't just any old village: it was built specially for the workers who build the royal tombs in the Valley of the Kings. Most Egyptian children learn about the world from helping their parents more and more as they get older, until they can do their job or look after the house. Farmers' kids help gather corn, while tomb-painters' kids might mix paints for their dads. There's no such thing as a careers advisor to help you find out what you want to be when you grow up — you'll do whatever job your dad does, and be grateful! In Deir el-Medina, the boys who work hardest and show most talent get to be the Children of the Tomb, which sounds pretty scary. Actually, it's a good thing: it means they join in with the work gangs and get trained up for a job.

Meryre's dad's a sculptor, so poor old Meryre gets to chip away at bits of stone all day.

Come on – we'll see if we can find any kids who aren't at work. There are often classes going on in the temples round here – if we sit at the back and don't get noticed, we can practise our hieroglyphs.

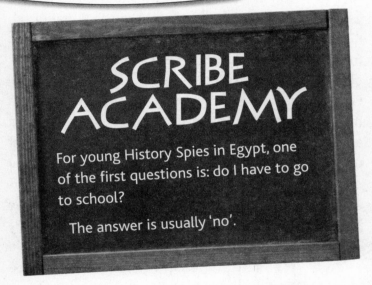

SCRIBE ACADEMY

For young History Spies in Egypt, one of the first questions is: do I have to go to school?

The answer is usually 'no'.

For starters, if you're a girl, you definitely won't go to school – hardly any girls learn to read or write. Of course, your History Spy training will mean you can read and write in the Egyptian language, but girls must remember to keep these skills under wraps – this can be a useful trick, as you could find yourself trusted with secrets people think you can't read. If you're undercover as a rich girl, you might have been taught to sing, dance and play music, so make sure you learn a bit of these skills before you go to Egypt.

In fact, there are only a few lucky people who get to learn to read and write: the scribes. Being a scribe isn't just a job. It makes you part of a whole separate class of people, and like other jobs, it's passed down from father to son. Even extremely rich, successful people like to have statues made of themselves with bits of papyrus on their laps and writing brushes in their hands, to show off their skills with words.

So even though I couldn't build a pyramid or even make the bread for dinner, just because I can read and write all the Egyptians would think I'm dead clever!

The village of Deir el-Medina is a special place, because of all the educated people who live there to work on the royal tombs. Here, most of the boys go to school for some of the time. They start going when they're five years old. Most of the time, they learn to write by copying out letters, words, and later whole stories. Thinking for yourself, and wishy-washy creative writing, are not encouraged.

And you'd better pay attention, because if the teacher thinks you're making too many mistakes he's likely to hit you! There's a saying in Egypt that 'boys have ears on their backs; they listen when they're beaten.'

> Here, take this bit of pot – we're supposed to be copying these hieroglyphs on to it.

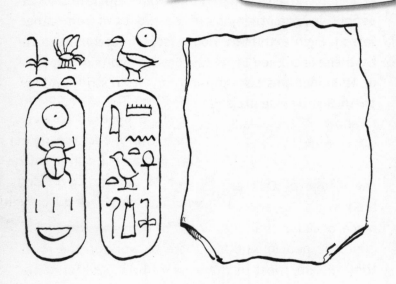

And that's just Tutankhamen's name! Just imagine if you had to write all that out every time you had to sign something! By the time you'd written a letter, all the news in it would be out of date.

Because hieroglyphs are so fiddly, the Egyptians have another kind of writing which they use for everyday notes, letters and accounts. It's called 'hieratic', and although it's simpler and quicker, some kids find it harder to learn than hieroglyphs, because at least hieroglyphs are drawn to look like something!

Once kids have spent a while copying words on to bits of old pot, they can move on to something more expensive: papyrus. We get our English word 'paper' from papyrus, which is the name of a reed that grows by the side of the Nile in Ancient Egypt.

The Egyptians cut it up into very thin strips and lay them side by side like this:

Next, they lay another layer over the top like this:

And finally, they sprinkle on a bit of water, bash it very hard with a hammer (so that all the plant juices help glue it flat together) and leave it to dry.

Papyrus is very handy for all kinds of writing – if you stick lots of bits together, you can roll it up into a scroll and write a novel that's as long as you want.

Maths is another lesson you need to pay attention in if you want to be a scribe. They don't do anything complicated, but scribes have to keep records of all sorts of things – how much the painters have been paid, how many jars of beer have been brewed, and how many cows someone owns. So they must be able to add up.

ADVENTURES OF ANCIENT EGYPT

Some of the books which scribes have to copy out are more exciting than dull old lists of cows and wages. The Egyptians have some great adventure stories too. You can read them to yourself on papyrus scrolls, but if your hieroglyph reading's a bit slow or if you're bored and missing your DVDs and soaps, seek out a storyteller. Here is the plot of an Egyptian bestseller.

The Story of the Shipwrecked Sailor: Never Lose Hope

A sailor loses his ship and all his friends in a big storm at sea. A wave washes him up on a desert island, far from home. Luckily, he meets a giant golden snake who speaks to him. The snake tells him how all his snake family were killed in a fire, and the sailor should be happy because in four months' time a boat is going to come and rescue him, and take him back to his wife and kids. True enough, the boat turns up, and the magic snake sends the sailor away with a boatload of pricey perfumes, ivory, dogs and monkeys.

Right . . . I think I'd have to have been on my own for quite a while before I started listening to magic talking snakes!

81

HIEROGLYPHIC HEADLINES

If anyone's likely to know the latest news from around Egypt and abroad, it's a scribe – they're the only ones who can send and read letters from faraway places. Here's the latest news from 1333:

MESOPOTAMIAN MARVELS

Of course, there's nowhere in the world that's quite as great as Egypt – but Mesopotamia comes close. They've had cities even longer than we have, and we've been trading with them for as long as we can remember. Right now, the warlike Hittites are just about to take charge, with their nippy little two-wheeled chariots. Let's hope they stay at home and don't come bothering us.

EGYPT RULES NUBIA, OK?

This is where we buy all the exotic animals and goodies that we love so much. Traders in Nubia can get you monkeys, giraffes, ostrich feathers, ivory and gold. We like it so much, we took it over. Since Pharaoh Thutmose III conquered it about a hundred years ago,

Egypt's been ruling Nubia too, and now we have gold mines there which are making us very rich indeed.

BOY KING TO VISIT THEBES

Our young Pharaoh Tutankhamen is due to be in the Thebes area next week, to take part in the annual festival of Opet. Royal-watchers say this year's Opet will be the biggest yet, as Tut settles into his reign and gets friendlier with the old gods of Egypt who his wicked dad rejected. Thousands of people are expected to turn up to gawp at the Pharaoh.

Sounds like a good party!

THE BIG BOAT PARTY

Opet is one of the biggest religious festivals in Egypt just now. It's celebrated every year when the Nile is flooding, and goes on for weeks.

Usually the statues of Egyptian gods stay locked inside their temples where only the priests are allowed in to see them. But lots of Egyptian festivals are based on the god coming out of his temple for a wander round, so the people can get a look at him and pray to him in person. At Opet, it's the great sun god Amun who gets to come out to play and to give Pharaoh his powers again for another year. The priests bring Amun's statue out of the temple, covered in posh clothes and bright jewellery, and riding on a sacred boat called a barque. They carry him down to the water and put him on to a real barge, so that he and the Pharaoh can travel

Priests carry the sacred boats on their shoulders.

The mighty Pharaoh Tutankhamen – at only eleven years old or so, he probably weighs a lot less than the statues.

This man has a question he wants to ask the great god.

up the river together and get to Luxor, where you're now standing. They're followed by another barge which carries the statues of the gods Mut and Khonsu, Amun's wife and son. All the way, crowds come out to watch the barges being pulled along – sometimes by boats, and sometimes by teams of men who walk along the banks dragging the barges on long ropes. Once they reach Luxor, the priests take the barques out of the boats and carry them on their shoulders up to the temple.

The god Amun – DON'T say it's just a statue. To Egyptians, it's the god himself as well!

Here they come! Quick, duck through to the front – we don't want to miss this!

Sem priests are the ones wearing leopard skins, and they lead the ordinary priests in the procession.

Dancers from Nubia – it is a party, after all.

YOUR PRAYERS ANSWERED

Lots of people ask questions when they pray. You can probably think of a few things you'd like to know the answer to. How can I get rich? What's the meaning of life? When's dinner? But even if you do ask things like that, you might not expect an answer, or at best you might hope God would give you a sign somehow. In Ancient Egypt, if you ask a god a question, you can expect a straight answer.

At Opet, you can go up and ask Amun a question while the priests are carrying his statue. If the answer's 'no', Amun's sacred boat will dip backwards. If it's a 'yes', the boat will move forward. Simple! Just remember only to ask questions with a yes or no answer – if you ask the one about the meaning of life, you'll just confuse everyone.

What d'you think? Impressive, isn't it? Imagine being Tutankhamen and having all those people staring at you, and being treated like a god! If he was back in our time he'd just be worrying the's running the country.

GODS, GODS & MORE GODS

The Egyptians have plenty of gods to worship. They've all got different jobs to do: some of them live in a particular town, and some of them look after particular people or things. Lots of them don't even look human! Depending on when you're visiting Egypt, different gods will be more or less powerful – for instance, the king's favourite god is always pretty important. Make sure you know a bit about all these gods, like every real Egyptian would.

AMUN: A sun god. His home is in Thebes, and he's Top God at the moment. That's partly because Tutankhamen's family comes from Thebes, and partly because the sun's so strong in Egypt!

RE : Another version of the sun god, also known as Ra and lots of other names besides. Re dies every sunset, but it's OK – he gets born again at dawn every day and gets to travel across the sky in a boat all over again.

HORUS : A sky god. Sometimes he's a falcon, sometimes a man with the head of a falcon.

TAWERET : A strange mix of lioness, hippo and crocodile, who looks after mothers and babies.

PTAH : Head god of the city of Memphis, Ptah is also the god who looks after craftsmen. They love him in the village of Deir el-Medina, where so many people are craftsmen working on the tombs.

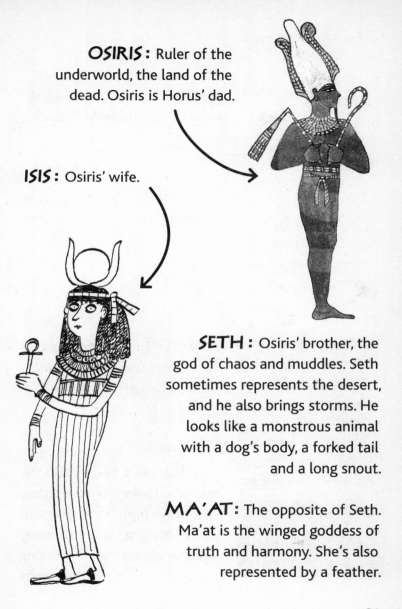

OSIRIS : Ruler of the underworld, the land of the dead. Osiris is Horus' dad.

ISIS : Osiris' wife.

SETH : Osiris' brother, the god of chaos and muddles. Seth sometimes represents the desert, and he also brings storms. He looks like a monstrous animal with a dog's body, a forked tail and a long snout.

MA'AT : The opposite of Seth. Ma'at is the winged goddess of truth and harmony. She's also represented by a feather.

ANUBIS: The jackal-headed god of embalming dead people.

HAPY: The fat man who represents the flooding of the Nile.

THOTH: The god of wisdom and scribes. He looks like either a baboon, an ibis (a kind of bird with a long beak) or a man with an ibis head.

> Weird. If I was drawing the god of wisdom, I definitely wouldn't pick a baboon!

GEB: The earth, shown as a man.

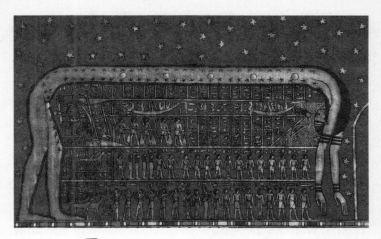

NUT : The sky, shown as a woman who stretches over the world in a bridge shape.

SEKHMET : A woman with the head of a lioness. She's a fierce goddess who helps the king out in battles.

MERETSEGER : A local snake goddess who lives in the mountains above Deir el-Medina. She looks after farming and the harvest.

WAYS TO PRAY

Popping along to a festival to get your once-a-year glimpse of the statue of a god is probably the most fun way to worship an Egyptian god. It's also a great time for History Spies to observe ordinary Egyptians, overhear news and gossip, and find out what sort of things people want to ask the gods. You won't see much in a big temple unless you're in disguise as a priest, and agents will need months of special training for that. Luckily, there are small shrines and local temples in towns and villages where you can go to pray alongside everyone else. People also keep small statues of the gods at home, so they can fit in a quick prayer between the housework and bedtime.

Remember to take food when you go to pray. Egyptian gods need to eat like everyone else, so you should always take offerings to leave in front of the god's statue.

Even better, why not make a holiday out of your religion? Because there are different gods all over Egypt and abroad, Egyptians who can afford it like to go travelling to pray to a far-off god. There are all sorts of plus points to this. You get to have a nice break and see a new city; you get the good luck that comes from praying to another god, who might do you favours that

It's a postcard from cousin Nakht — he's been on another god-finding holiday.

TEMPLE OF HAPY

your usual gods haven't got round to yet; and you get to show off to all your friends back home about what a lovely holiday you've had. Of course, there's another reason why History Spies like this kind of holiday. Agents who are only in a city for a few days often disguise themselves as pilgrims. It explains any strange accent you might have, or little mistakes you make when you're chatting.

I don't think that would work for us. Not many people would believe two kids would be allowed to go off on their own to pray to a foreign god — or even that we'd want to.

NOT A GOD –
THE GOD !

Things have been a bit sticky for the gods recently. The Pharaoh in charge a few years before Tutankhamen was called Akhenaten – he was probably Tut's dad, but we don't know for sure. Akhenaten had a very strange idea about religion. He decided that most of the gods that Egyptians had worshipped for thousands of years weren't actually important, and everyone should worship just one god.

You're all out of a job!

The god he picked was the Aten, a sun god that was shown as a golden disc. He also insisted that the only way to pray to Aten was through the Pharaoh, making himself even more important. Akhenaten even built a whole new city in the desert where he could pray to the Aten, and he changed his name along with his god – Akhenaten means 'the goodness of the Aten'. Even Tutankhamen wasn't born with that name – he grew up being called Tutankhaten, which means 'the living image of the Aten'. But the Egyptian people weren't all that keen on suddenly having one lonely god, and they didn't forget all the old gods. So a couple of years after Tutankhaten got to be Pharaoh, he moved out of the city in the desert, changed his name to Tutankhamen (for Amun, the other sun god), and brought all the old gods back again. So this Opet is a very happy one, because people are glad to have things back to normal again.

Psst – Charlie! Want to see something really exciting? Take this – but be very careful, and you HAVE to keep it a secret! Good luck!

Use this key to work out what the hieroglyphs say.

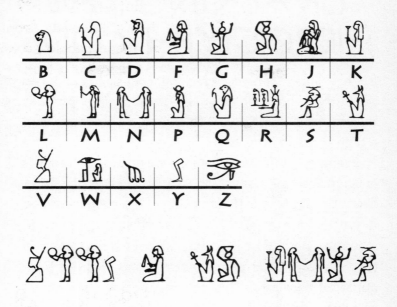

B	C	D	F	G	H	J	K

L	M	N	P	Q	R	S	T

V	W	X	Y	Z

Amazing! That makes this is a totally top-secret document. No one's supposed to know where some of these tombs are, to stop them getting burgled, but Meryre must have found out while he was at work. Well? Are you brave enough to go and have a look round once it gets dark? We can't miss a spying chance like this.

Solution: VLLY F TH KNGS

CRACKING THE HIEROGLYPH CODE

History Spies who like cracking codes should know the story of how the language of the hieroglyphs was rediscovered – with a visit to church, an old stone, and a slightly weird little boy.

Eventually, once the Pharaohs are no longer in charge in Egypt and Egyptians start using other kinds of writing, like Latin and Arabic, the meaning of hieroglyphs will be forgotten for a long time. All those Pharaohs who made sure their names were written all over their tombs so they'd always be remembered might as well not have bothered, because the hieroglyphs become just a bunch of pretty little pictures. But centuries later, European travellers will get excited about the mysteries of the Pyramids and want to know who built them. The secrets, they decide, must be hidden in the hieroglyphs.

For years, the European eggheads who try to decode hieroglyphs go about it the wrong way. They think that all those little symbols are magical signs, instead of an alphabet that tells you what a word should sound like. The other problem is that no one speaks Ancient Egyptian any more – so if they did work out what a word sounded like, they still couldn't tell what it meant.

Until, that is, in the 1600s a German priest says that maybe the strange language that's still used in Christian churches in Egypt is the same as the language the Ancient Egyptians spoke. Amazingly, he's right. But he still can't decode the hieroglyphs, because he can't know which Egyptian words are on the bit of papyrus he's looking at.

The next big clue comes in 1799, when the British and French armies are fighting over who gets to be in charge of Egypt. A troop of French soldiers are clearing out an old fort called Rosetta so they can fight off the British, when they come across a big flat stone with writing all over it. Three different kinds of writing, in fact: hieroglyphs, Egyptian everyday letters, and Ancient Greek.

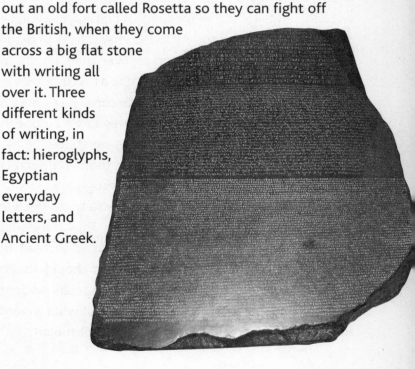

Well, all well-educated Europeans speak Greek in the 1700s, so finally they've found a piece of hieroglyphic writing AND they know what it's supposed to mean.

The clues are in place, but it will still take a brainy and very hard-working man to come up with the answer. Jean-François Champollion grows up in France in the 1790s, when Egypt is all the rage. He's fascinated by it, and becomes totally obsessed with cracking the code of the hieroglyphs. His parents probably hope it's a strange phase that he'll grow out of when he starts getting interested in girls. But no, he keeps on trying. He learns Ancient Egyptian, and he reads all the hieroglyphs he can get his hands on. Then one day, in 1822, he works out that this ...

means Ramses.

His big idea is that some of the hieroglyphs are symbols (like O, the sign for the sun god Ra) ...

...and some of them are just sound-signs (like the letter S).

With all the knowledge he's been collecting since he was a kid, he whips up a dictionary of hieroglyphs in no time. When he's a grown-up in his late thirties, he finally gets to go to Egypt and see it for himself. He can read all the hieroglyphs on the monuments he goes to see – and he's the first person in hundreds of years who can.

Come on then – we should get going. I want to see the tombs of the dead Pharaohs! The Valley of the Kings is this way – follow me.

HOW TO LIVE FOREVER

Even before History Spy training, most of you will know something about how the Ancient Egyptians made their dead into mummies so that they could live forever. The Egyptians' strange beliefs about the afterlife are famous. Here's what any Egyptian would want to happen to them after they die. History Spies with a strong stomach could try getting a job as an embalmer's assistant, to help us find out more about this interesting process. This is how we think it's done.

HOW TO MAKE A MUMMY

● Put the body on a sturdy table. Make sure it's a wipe-clean surface.

● Remove the brain. Brains decay and go runny quite quickly after death, so if you make a hole through the nose and wiggle a metal hook around inside, it should come out easily. Throw the brain away – Egyptian doctors believe it's only useful for pumping snot into the nose.

> OK, I think I might be sick. And I like disgusting things!

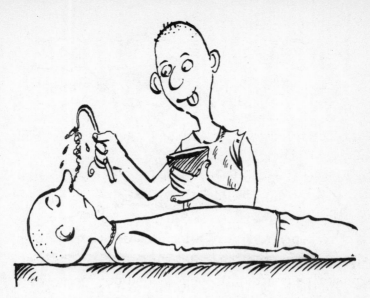

- Cut the belly open and take out all the innards apart from the heart, which Egyptians believe is where a person's mind and soul is. Be very careful with the liver, lungs, stomach and intestines. Put these aside and we'll deal with them shortly.

- Swish some palm wine around the inside of the body to clean it – it gets rid of unpleasant smells, and the alcohol in the wine will kill germs.

- Take the innards you put aside just now. Clean and dry them, then cover them with melted resin and wrap them in strips of linen cloth. Put them in their special jars, which will be buried next to the body.

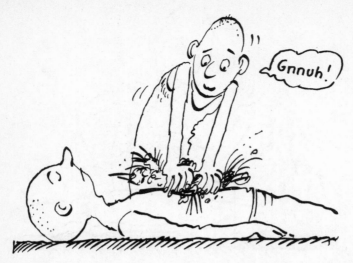

- Fill the body with dry stuffing so it keeps its shape.

- Put the body on a sloping board, cover it completely with natron (a kind of salt), and leave it there for forty days. When you come back, the natron will have soaked up all the moisture and dried out the body completely – this is extremely important to stop it from rotting.

- Clean off the natron, and take out the stuffing from the body.

- Pack the body again with clean stuffing. You can use linen, sawdust, or even soil. Some embalmers like to bung in a few onions, for their nice smell.

- Close over the hole you made in the belly with a piece of wax or metal.

- Rub some perfume into the body.

- Seal up the nose and mouth, and put pads of linen over the eyeballs.

- Rub the skin all over with molten resin, to seal and preserve it.

- Now for the arty part. Take a lot of long linen bandages, and start wrapping the mummy up very carefully. Start with the fiddly bits, like fingers and toes. In between the bandages you should put as many bits of jewellery and magical trinkets

as the dead person's family can afford. If you're mummifying a king, don't hold back! Tutankhamen will have bracelets, rings, necklaces, jewellery for his fingers and toes, and loads of protective amulets wrapped up in his bandages when it's his turn.

You're all set. Now the mummy can be put in a series of coffins like a Russian doll, buried in its tomb, and left to spend the rest of time having a lovely afterlife – all thanks to you.

You might end up thinking that the Egyptians are obsessed with death, what with all the effort they put into looking after dead people. But actually, they do all this because they really love being alive, and they want to carry on that way. They think the afterlife will be like this one but with all the unpleasant bits taken out, and only good food, good weather, fun games and parties to enjoy for ever after.

Carved stone sarcophagus

MULTI~PURPOSE MUMMIES

The Ancient Egyptians treat mummies with huge respect. After all, to them, mummies are still people who are going to be alive again sooner or later. But give it a few hundred years and people will start digging up mummies and using them for all kinds of strange things.

CENTRAL HEATING: Wood doesn't grow well in Egypt and sometimes it can get chilly at night. So, in a couple of thousand years' time, some Egyptians get tempted to chuck a papery old mummy on the fire to keep warm.

PAINT: Artists will do anything to get the look they're after – even crumble up someone's dead gran. In Europe in the 1500s, there was a particular shade of brown paint called mummy. It was specially imported all the way from Egypt and made from – you guessed it – ground-up mummy.

PILLS: In medieval Europe, medical textbooks recommend bitumen for some diseases. And people believe that Egyptian mummies are covered in bitumen, and that's what gives them that sticky black sheen. Actually, Egyptian embalmers don't use bitumen at all, but because of the big mix-up medieval Europeans start buying old Egyptian mummies and turning them into pills and potions. Francis I, who's King of France in the 1500s, is one of the celebs who thinks a mummy a day keeps the doctor away – every morning he takes a bit of rhubarb with a spoonful of mummy powder.

Because of this, the mummies that modern archaeologists have to study are only a tiny fraction of all the bodies which were mummified in Egypt. So even though mummies last a very long time, History Spies can and should bring back valuable information about them, because many mummies will be lost later on.

Yuck! My mum just makes me take multivitamins – I'm so glad someone invented those!

OK, we're here. The Valley of the Kings, the last resting place of the Egyptian royals. And now it's dark, the workmen have gone home and we should be able to sneak around. There could be guards around though, so keep dead quiet and we'll double-check there's no one here before we use a torch.

You're not scared, are you? I'm not – no way. Definitely not. What's scary about a few dead people?

THE MUMMY'S CURSE

A mouldering mummy has been a favourite monster in horror films for years. After all, ghosts and zombies are scary, and the whole point of a mummy is that they're a dead person who's supposed to live forever!

You probably know that if you break into an Egyptian tomb, you'll be cursed by the mummy and die a horrible death. But is it true? Should agents really be afraid of being cursed in Egypt? The most famous mummy's curse is Tutankhamen's.

When Howard Carter and the Earl of Carnarvon open Tut's tomb on 26 November 1922, all kinds of scary rumours fly around the world:

- The day the tomb is opened, Carter's pet canary is swallowed whole by a cobra. The cobra, of course, is the sacred snake which protects the Pharaohs of Egypt.

- Four months later, Lord Carnarvon himself dies. He comes down with a fever after a mosquito bite gets infected. At the exact same moment he dies, his little dog Susie lets out a sad howl and also drops dead – and all the lights go out in Cairo.

- An X-ray expert travels from England to examine Tut's mummy – but he dies before he even gets to Egypt.

● A famous rich American called Jay Gould dies of pneumonia, after catching cold on a trip round Tut's tomb.

Spooky stuff. But if they *are* the victims of the mummy's curse, then Tutankhamen is either a bit confused or just not very good at cursing. Howard Carter, the first man to enter the tomb, lives for another seventeen years, and the doctor who cut up Tutankhamen's body to examine it survives another forty-seven years and dies at the grand old age of eighty-seven.

In fact, no archaeologists have ever found any writing in an Egyptian tomb to say, 'Keep out, or you'll be cursed and die a horrible death.' This is one danger History Spies *don't* have to worry about.

Now, on Meryre's map it says there's a way in just here . . . Aha, got it! Follow me, and quickly, in case anyone's around.

Wow! I'm not sure whose tomb this is, but it's got to be someone royal. This place is FULL of stuff!

PACKING FOR A VERY LONG TRIP

Because the Egyptians hope that each person they bury will live forever, they make sure they've got all the things they might need with them. That's why you'll see all these things packed into an Egyptian tomb:

Food: all sorts of tasty titbits, including ducks, bread, cakes, peas, honey, dates and nuts

Little statues called **shabtis** *– in the afterlife, they'll be your servants and do any chores that need doing*

Make-up: because dead people want to look good too

Linen clothes

Wigs and sandals: you can never have too many accessories

Lamps: you'll need to see where you're going, obviously

If it was me, I'd want some decent computer games if I had to sit here for the whole of eternity. Oh, and a big heap of chocolate biscuits!

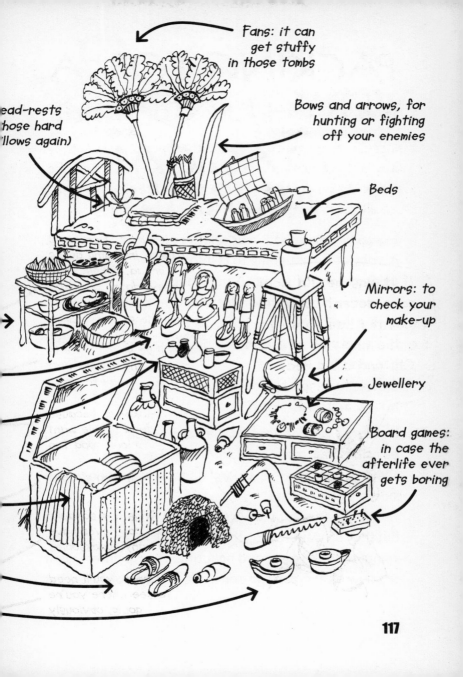

Fans: it can get stuffy in those tombs

Bows and arrows, for hunting or fighting off your enemies

ead-rests
hose hard
llows again)

Beds

Mirrors: to check your make-up

Jewellery

Board games: in case the afterlife ever gets boring

Wow – take the torch! These pictures on the walls are amazing!

MAGICAL MURALS

However much food your relatives leave in your tomb, it's obviously not going to last forever. Tomb decorators paint scenes of farming and hunting on to the walls of tombs, so that in the afterlife the dead person will always be able to get more to eat. Painting a picture of something on a wall is a bit like a spell to make it happen.

Draw Yourself Egyptian:

Have you ever noticed that all the people in Egyptian paintings look really similar? Are the Egyptians really all slim and triangle-shaped, and do they walk everywhere sideways, like crabs?

Of course not – you've seen them up close yourself! But they do want to look the same in pictures – everyone wants to look young and beautiful. Their painters want to show all the parts of someone's body, not just what it looks like from one angle. If you're working as an artist on your History Spy mission, you'll need to know how it's done. Practise: try drawing yourself, a friend, an aunt or Batman, using the same method the Ancient Egyptians used.

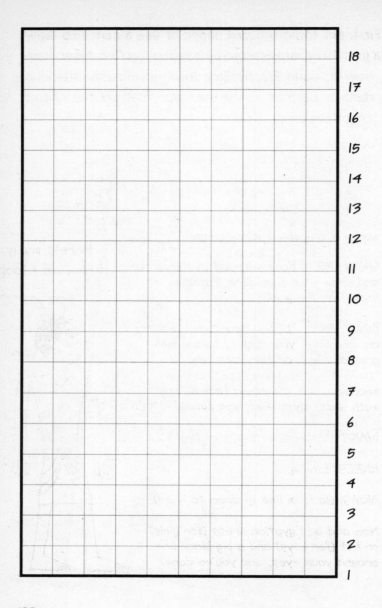

18

17

16

15

14

13

12

11

10

9

8

7

6

5

4

3

2

1

First, get some squared paper, or use a pencil to draw a grid 18 squares tall and 10 squares across. Now draw yourself, bit by bit, but pay attention to the following rules:

FACE: Two squares in height. Draw the shape of your face side on. Harder if you're drawing yourself, but you could work from a photo, or get a friend to help.

EYES: You'll only see one, because you're only drawing one side of your face. But make sure you draw it as it looks in the mirror, not as it looks from the side! Don't worry if it looks a funny shape.

SHOULDERS: Face yourself in the mirror and draw your shoulders. Put them at line 15 on the grid.

BODY, ARMS, LEGS: Now turn sideways on, and draw your chest, tummy, hips, arms and legs as they look now. This is why Egyptians look like triangles: because their shoulders face on are much wider than their hips sideways on.

WAIST: Make sure this is at line 10.

KNEES: Line 6.

ARMS: Go from line 15 down to line 9.

Now add an Egyptian dress (for girls) or kilt (for boys) and a big black line around your eyes, and you're done!

Here's my go – how do I look?

THE ROUGH GUIDE TO BEING DEAD

Egyptians can't just rely on being mummified to get them into the afterlife. Dead people have work to do too! That's why tombs and pyramids often have papyrus guidebooks inside them. The 'Book of the Dead' tells the dead person what to expect when they reach the underworld.

There are all sorts of things they'll have to do, spells to remember, and questions they'll have to answer in the right way. The scariest part is when they get judged by the god Osiris, to see whether they were naughty or nice when they were alive.

This scene is often painted on the walls of tombs, to help make sure it happens. The dead person's heart is put on one side of a pair of scales, and on the other side is Ma'at, the goddess of truth, who sometimes appears as a feather. The god Thoth is standing by waiting to see what happens and write it down.

Also nearby is a vicious monster called the Devourer. If the person's heart weighs less than Ma'at, then he did too many bad things in his lifetime, and the Devourer gets to gobble up the heart for dinner. And that means no afterlife for the poor dead person. If he's been good though, he'll get his heart back and can head on up to the afterlife.

Eww, look at this picture! There's a horrible monster, and I think that blob's supposed to be someone's heart!

GRAVE ROBBERS

The problem with stuffing tombs so full of valuables is that they're very tempting to burglars. Most of the royal tombs in the Valley of the Kings get burgled at some point. The reason Tutankhamen's tomb is so famous is that it's one of the few that will make it to modern times without having been cleared out.

Tomb robbery's always a problem in ancient Egypt. Often, someone who works on the tombs will go back and take something when no one's around. After all, they know all the ways in and where the good stuff is! Tomb robbery is a very serious crime. The Egyptians don't just fill their tombs with goodies for the sake of it – if you steal from a tomb, you're stealing from a dead person who still needs their stuff!

Even worse, many robbers unwrap the mummies in the tombs they burgle. They're after all the jewellery that's wrapped up inside the bandages. Once that's done, they often burn the mummies. That means that archaeologists won't be able to find anything out from that mummy later on. But more importantly for the Egyptians, the dead person's afterlife is over – and if he was a king, he won't be able to hang out with the gods and keep Egypt safe any more!

Because tomb robbery is such a dreadful crime, the builders of the tombs try putting in security features. Some tombs have deep pits for robbers to fall into, or corridors that look like dead ends. But the robbers still get in.

One thing which might make a potential tomb robber think twice is the punishment they could get. Some of them get their noses and ears cut off, or are sent out of the country forever. But the ultimate punishment for tomb robbery is truly horrible: execution by being lowered on to a pointy stick and pierced through the belly.

Oh yuck! If anyone catches us here, they'll think **we're** robbers – and I really don't fancy meeting one of those spikes!

SPOT THE BURGLARS' BOOTY

Compare this picture with the one on page 117. What's missing? You'll find the answers over the page.

Robbers go for anything portable and expensive. Here's what they took out of this room:

- Clothes: Linen cloth is valuable, it all looks pretty much the same so it's hard to tell if it's stolen, and it's easy to carry.

- Make-up: If the tomb's not too old, the make-up in it might still be good. It's precious stuff, and worth taking.

- Gold jewellery: Anything metal is a good find for tomb robbers, because they can melt it down and turn it into something else.

- Head-rest: This one's made of ivory, which comes from far-off parts of Africa and is very valuable.

They've gone further in – let's get out of here, but be careful not to knock anything over!

Oh blimey! More people! Duck behind this wall, quick – and let's hope they're not after us!

THE MENACING MEDJAY

Instead of policemen, the Egyptians have bands of scary soldiers called the Medjay. The Medjay were a tribe who used to live in the desert and come down to work for the Egyptian army every now and then, and for the last few hundred years they've been living in Egypt permanently and working as policemen. These days, 'Medjay' just means the police. One unit of Medjay is responsible for guarding the Valley of the Kings. If the Medjay catch

you committing a crime, you can be hauled up in front
of the court and given all sorts of punishments, from
being hit a hundred times with a cane, to having your
hand cut off, being forced to work down a mine, or even
being beheaded, burned alive, or impaled on a spike.

They're heading into the tomb – those robbers are
for it now! It's definitely time to get out of here, if
we don't want to be made into kebabs along with
them. Touch the annostat again and let's get home . . .

That was close! I'm not going to go hanging around
in tombs again in a hurry. Turns out there's a lot
more to be scared of than just ghosts! I'm not going
to complain about being bored for a while – it's just
nice to be home where it's safe.

130

TIME MAP

It's sometimes hard to work out which year you should be visiting – the Department is still working out exactly when things happened in Ancient Egypt. Use these rough dates as a guide, but be prepared to hop around a bit if you've travelled to the wrong year. And always make notes to help us become more accurate!

We measure out Egyptian history in the time its kings reigned for. A group of kings make a dynasty, and there are several dynasties in each bigger chunk of time, called either a kingdom or a period.

3100–2613BC EARLY DYNASTIC PERIOD

3100–2890	The First Dynasty of Egyptian kings.
3000	Earliest hieroglyphs are written down.
2686–2613	Third Dynasty. In this dynasty, the first pyramid is built at Saqqara – it's not quite a true pyramid, because the sides go up in steps instead of smoothly.

2613–2125 OLD KINGDOM (4TH–8TH DYNASTIES)

2613–2494	Fourth Dynasty including Khufu (Cheops). These kings build the Great Pyramids and the Great Sphinx of Giza.

2160–2040 FIRST INTERMEDIATE PERIOD (9TH–11TH DYNASTIES)

Egypt splits into two kingdoms, the north and the south.

1975–1640 MIDDLE KINGDOM (11TH–14TH DYNASTIES)

Ancient Egyptian art and literature develops its style.

1630–1520 SECOND INTERMEDIATE PERIOD (15TH–17TH DYNASTIES)

The Hyksos, a bunch of warlike foreigners, move in and rule Egypt. They bring with them little chariots and other clever inventions, which the Egyptians find handy.

1539–1075 NEW KINGDOM (18TH–20TH DYNASTIES)

1550–1295 Eighteenth Dynasty.

1525–1504 Reign of Pharaoh Amenhotep I, who starts work on the Valley of the Kings.

1479–1457 Reign of Hatshepsut, the bearded female Pharaoh.

1352–1336 Reign of Amenhotep IV, the Pharaoh who changes his name to Akhenaten to honour his favourite god. Akhenaten is probably Tutankhamen's dad.

1336–1327   Tutankhamen is Pharaoh of Egypt. He's only eight or nine years old when he becomes king.

Robbers break into Tutankhamen's tomb soon after it's sealed, and take some make-up – but, luckily for archaeologists, not much else.

1327–1323   Ay, who was Tut's advisor, gets to be Pharaoh.

1323–1295   Pharaoh Horemheb reigns.

1279–1213   Reign of Ramses II, the busy Pharaoh who's known as Ramses the Great! He fights the Hittites, signs the world's first ever peace treaty, and has over 100 sons.

1075–715   THIRD INTERMEDIATE PERIOD (21ST–24TH DYNASTIES)

715–332   LATE PERIOD (25TH–30TH DYNASTIES, 2ND PERSIAN PERIOD)

332 BC–395 AD GRECO-ROMAN PERIOD (MACEDONIANS, PTOLEMIES AND ROMANS)

332–323   Alexander the Great rules Egypt. For the next thousand years, Egypt will be ruled by Greek speakers.

196   The Rosetta Stone is carved with the words of priests praising the Pharaoh Ptolemy V.

51–30   Cleopatra rules Egypt.

30   The Roman Emperor Octavian conquers Egypt and makes it part of the Roman Empire.

MODERN ERA

1799   French soldiers discover the Rosetta Stone, the key to unlocking the hieroglyph code.

1824   Code fanatic Jean-François Champollion publishes his guide to reading hieroglyphs.

1922   Howard Carter discovers the tomb of Tutankhamen and the long-dead teenager becomes an overnight celebrity all over again.

Back to the Blitz

HISTORY SPIES

Have you ever been on a top-secret, life-and-death, time-bending government mission before?

Liverpool: 1940

The war is raging and the Department of Historical Accuracy need a brave and daring History Spy to uncover the truth...

Your mission: learn how to identify enemy aircraft, make spitfires out of saucepans and disguise yourself as an evacuee. Find out how people spoke, what they ate, and become a champion at marbles!

Join top History Spy Charlie Cartwright in his adventures as he travels through space and time, dodging bombs, dinosaurs and erupting volcanoes.

ESCAPE FROM VESUVIUS

HISTORY SPIES

Have you ever been on a top-secret, life-and-death, time-bending government mission before?

Pompeii: AD 79

Vesuvius is about to erupt and the Department of Historical Accuracy needs a History Spy with nerves of steel ...

Your mission: find out what went on at a gladiator battle, why it's OK to burp at a banquet and why everyone in Pompeii was so smelly! Then, if you're brave enough, you can check out the eruption that buried the city for 2,000 years.

Join top History Spy Charlie Cartwright in his adventures as he travels through space and time, dodging bombs, dinosaurs and erupting volcanoes.

The Great Exhibition Mission

HISTORY SPIES

Have you ever been on a top-secret, life-and-death, time-bending government mission before?

London: 1851

Queen Victoria is on the throne. It's the year of the Great Exhibition. The Department of Historical Accuracy needs an adventurous History Spy to get the facts straight ...

Your mission: learn how to think, speak and dress like a Victorian and go and explore the streets of London. Find out about the fearsome factories, dinosaur bones and incredible inventions that made the Victorian age so exciting ...

Join top History Spy Charlie Cartwright in his adventures as he travels through space and time, dodging bombs, dinosaurs and erupting volcanoes.

A selected list of titles available from Macmillan Children's Books

The prices shown below are correct at the time of going to press. However, Macmillan Publishers reserves the right to show new retail prices on covers, which may differ from those previously advertised.

Jo Foster

History Spies: Back to the Blitz	978-0-330-44899-4	£4.99
History Spies:		
The Great Exhibition Mission	978-0-330-44001-4	£4.99
History Spies: Escape from Vesuvius	978-0-330-44900-7	£4.99

All Pan Macmillan titles can be ordered from our website, www.panmacmillan.com, or from your local bookshop and are also available by post from:

Bookpost, PO Box 29, Douglas, Isle of Man IM99 1BQ

Credit cards accepted. For details:
Telephone: 01624 677237
Fax: 01624 670923
Email: bookshop@enterprise.net
www.bookpost.co.uk

Free postage and packing in the United Kingdom